CONTENTS

Colonialism, or the acquisition and control of another country in order to populate it and exploit its resources, has been around since ancient times. The Greeks used it when they expanded around the Mediterranean Sea; the Persians used it in the Middle East; and the Huns used it in Mongolia. These conquerors occupied neighboring territories as well as those thousands of miles away. In colonialism, people who live under foreign rule face special challenges. The controlling colonizers may deny the colony's inhabitants civil rights and a say in government.

The Age of Discovery began in the late fifteenth century, when Columbus and other Europeans sailed the oceans searching for faraway lands, whom they hoped to profit from. The discovery of the New World—the Americas—led to the establishment of the thirteen original British colonies on the east coast of North America. The French maintained a substantial presence in North America as well. The Spanish established footholds in Mexico that expanded into North America. They also controlled great swaths of territory in Central and South America.

India fell under British control by the eighteenth century. The Dutch seized lands in Indonesia, and the French took over the area called Indochina, which today is made up of Laos, Cambodia, Vietnam, and Thailand.

The word "colony" forms the basis of colonialism. Usually, a colony involves people who

THE COLONIES OF

NORTH AMERICA

at the

Declaration of Independence

In 1776, when the American colonies declared independence from Great Britain, the colonies looked different than they did at the start of colonization more than a century earlier.

live in a territory that is under the rule of a parent state. Colonies often developed alongside indigenous people who had their own culture and traditions. Inevitably, native peoples and colonists came to blows, usually to devastating effect.

Two features exist in colonies. One is that the colonizers establish power over subject peoples. The second is that colonizers take more from their colonies than they return.

European nations controlled more than half of the earth's surface at one time. The United States, born from thirteen British colonies, won its fight for independence more than two hundred years ago. Other countries have struggled longer and harder for the right to self-determination and freedom. Though most Latin American countries threw off colonial rule in the nineteenth century, the majority of colonized nations in Asia and Africa won their independence in the twentieth century. Yet European colonizers left a legacy of political, cultural, and governmental changes that continue to influence their former colonies to this day.

Former colonies often deal with a number of negative effects from their past, including loss of indigenous population from enslavement or disease, differences in class levels due to unequal access to education, an absence of resources that were taken by colonizers, and unstable governmental systems that have led to the rise of strongmen. Poverty and a lack of industrialization plague some former colonies while others, like Canada and the United States, have carved out a rich, prosperous society.

CHAPTER 1

REIGN OF THE SPANISH

When Italian explorer Christopher Columbus gained approval and assistance from the Spanish crown to search for a new trade route to the east, he felt certain that he would land on the shores of India. Instead, in 1492 he reached North and South America.

The ruins of Machu Picchu, which means "old peak" in the Incan language, is a deserted city that dates from the mid-1400s to the mid-1500s. It lies about 50 miles (80 kilometers) from Cuzco, Peru.

Colombus's first claim was the island of Hispaniola (the present-day Dominican Republic and Haiti) for Spain. Soon, the Spanish explored, conquered, and colonized many Caribbean islands and neighboring regions.

The Spanish conquistadors defeated the natives again and again despite being outnumbered, sometimes more than a hundred to one. They had superior weapons, including firearms, which native peoples had never seen. But the Europeans also exposed them to deadly diseases to which they had no immunity. In a terrifyingly short time, illness devastated the natives.

THE INCAN EMPIRE

At the time of the conquistadors, the Incas had an advanced and extensive empire. Based in present-day Peru, the empire extended nearly 2,500 miles (4,025 km) along the western coast of the South American continent. The Spanish crown sent Francisco Pizarro to claim for Spain the land south of Panama along the western coast. In 1531, with a force of a few hundred men, Pizarro easily captured the Inca emperor Atahuallpa, who had thirty thousand Inca warriors at his command. Subduing the Incas with advanced weapons, the Spanish spent the next few years cementing their hold, as they removed the riches of the Incan empire.

GOLD, GLORY, AND GOD

Once Spain controlled Mexico, large parts of South America, and the West Indies, the stage was set for the first wave of European colonialism. The Spanish and Portuguese wanted these lands because they thought they were rich in gold and silver. Both nations were heavily influenced by the Roman Catholic Church, which was a major political force in Europe at the time. The church decided to divide the known lands between the two countries.

In 1493, Pope Alexander VI issued the Inter Caetera. This papal bull, or decree of the church, was written at the request of King Ferdinand and Queen Isabella of Spain. It declared that the sacred mission of the explorers should be to convert the native people to Catholicism. Most people living in the Americas, like the Incas and Aztecs, were polytheistic. They worshipped many gods. The Spanish and Portuguese used the decree to justify conquering and controlling people who were not Christian. They considered indigenous people to be savages, inferior to Catholic Europeans. Because the Spanish and Portuguese thought that

The Treaty of Tordesillas is named after a city in Spain. The treaty had an important result: it is the reason why Brazilians speak Portuguese and much of the rest of Latin America speaks Spanish. See partial transcription on page 53.

God approved their actions, they were all the more eager to proceed with their quest.

After the church had divided the land, the Portuguese realized that they had gotten much less land than they expected. A year later, in 1494, the Treaty of Tordesillas was signed. The imaginary line was moved farther west. This would result in the Portuguese controlling the area that today is Brazil, while the Spanish took over most of the rest of South America.

THE ENCOMIENDA SYSTEM

The Spanish devised a system to split up their new territories. It was called encomienda, meaning "charge" or "mission." It was based on the feudal system of land grants that existed in Spain at the time. A Spaniard arriving in the New World was issued land. As the encomendero, this man ruled over a certain number

INCAN SOCIETY

Before the arrival of the Spanish, the Incas in Peru lived under a class system like many other societies. The Inca system was split into three parts. A small ruling class made the decisions for everyone. Below the rulers was a class of aristocrats, who were the managers and professionals. The third and lowest class was made up of laborers.

The Incas were reported to have had a social welfare system. Under their system, old and injured workers would be provided an income after they were unable to work. However, the rule of law in Inca society was also very strict. Under Inca law, a seemingly minor crime such as theft often carried a penalty of death.

of natives. The number depended on the size of the land granted to him by the Spanish crown.

Each encomendero was supposed to protect the Native Americans on his land. However, the natives were required to pay a tribute to the encomendero. The church also required the encomendero to Christianize his subjects.

The system of encomienda was supposed to improve most of the Native Americans and civilize them. However, many encomenderos treated them as subhuman slaves, a cheap source of labor.

In addition, the natives had no immunity to European diseases. Thousands died from illnesses carried by the Spanish. In addition, whether on plantations or in the harsh environments of mines where they were forced to dig for precious metals, subject Native Americans were literally worked to death.

The Spanish invaders were killing off their workers faster than they could be replaced. Administrators in the mother country, prodded by concerned missionaries, tried to reduce these abuses. With the great distance between Spain and the New World, it could take several weeks for instructions to reach the colonists. Often, people sent over to ensure that Spain's rules were followed became part of the problem themselves.

REFORM AND REVOLT

King Charles I of Spain passed the New Laws of 1542 that abolished Native American slavery. Meanwhile, the African slave trade to the West Indies remained in full swing.

Spanish settlers who abused their stations could have their encomiendas removed. No more encomiendas would be granted. Encomiendas could no longer be passed down from father to son. When an encomendero died, his encomienda reverted back to the Spanish king.

Cus CO.

CVSCO, REGNI PERV IN NOVO ORBE CAPVT.

This colored engraving from 1582 depicts the city of Cuzco, Peru. The engraving comes from the *Civitates Orbis Terrarum,* or Cities of the World, published as six volumes between 1572 and 1617.

The Spanish also set up the audiencia, a colonial government that would answer directly to the king and queen. Only members of the audiencia were allowed to distribute land. These new measures sought to rein in Spanish settlers who were especially brutal.

In Peru, the center of New Spain, the encomenderos were particularly worried about these laws. In 1541, Francisco Pizarro, who had been ruler of Peru, was killed during a property dispute between Spanish landholders. One of his brothers, Gonzalo Pizarro, led a revolt of landholders against the new administration.

In the end, the Spanish suspended the New Laws. The rebellion had cut off the flow of riches from New Spain to the mother country. Charles I sent Pedro de la Gasca as an emissary, or representative, to regain the support of the settlers.

De la Gasca met Gonzalo Pizarro in battle. On April 9, 1548, Pizarro and his followers were defeated, and Pizarro was executed.

Although the rule of the crown was reestablished, the encomienda system never really disappeared. In fact, many of those charged with getting rid of its worst abuses were themselves encomenderos. Spanish settlers, much like the people of the thirteen colonies of the United States, eventually rebelled against the crown. By the early half of the nineteenth century, Spain had lost all of its colonies in the Western Hemisphere, except for Cuba.

Times were changing. Other nations would enter the race for economic world dominance. In the coming centuries, British and European powers would hold sway over much of the earth's surface and change forever the lives of millions of people.

CHAPTER 2

THE BRITISH COME TO AMERICA

When British settlers claimed land in North America, they came face to face with the original owners, Native Americans. With them, the British unknowingly brought diseases of the Old World to infect the natives with illnesses to which they had no resistance. As Native Americans died in increasing numbers from these plagues, they also struggled to maintain their ancestral lands in the face of waves upon waves of European colonists.

A DIFFICULT BEGINNING

The first permanent British settlement in North America was Jamestown. Founded on May 14, 1607, on the coast of present-day Virginia, Jamestown struggled for its life right from the beginning. Starvation, illness, and bitter cold during the winter of 1610 reduced the original group of five hundred people to about sixty.

This lithograph from 1897 depicts captives who have just arrived from Africa. One is being auctioned off by the settlers who lived in early Jamestown, Virginia.

By 1617, the settlers had learned how to grow corn and tobacco. But there weren't enough people to farm effectively. In 1619, Jamestown settlers brought in white and black indentured servants who would earn their freedom after four to seven years of labor. Forty years later, Jamestown became the first American colony to create laws legalizing slavery.

As the British colonists pushed farther into the wilderness around Jamestown, they fought the Native Americans who inhabited these lands. Over time, Jamestown became the home of the wealthier members of the colony, while the frontier was inhabited by new, poor arrivals. It was mostly these newcomers who fought the natives, suffering the most from their counterattacks.

COLONIES OF NEW ENGLAND

North of Virginia, in present-day Massachusetts, a group of Puritan settlers landed at Plymouth Rock. They established the

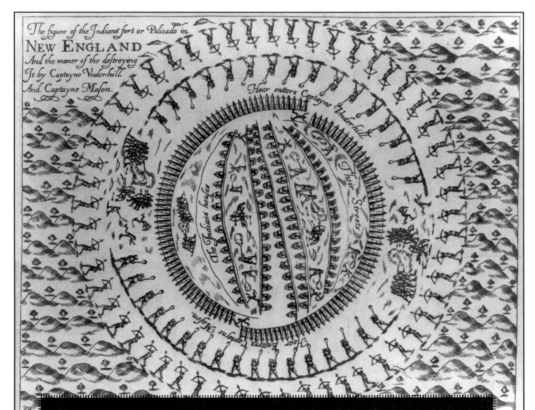

The title of this 1638 drawing is *The figure of the Indians' fort or palizado in New England and the manner of the destroying it by Captayne Underhill and Captayne Mason*. It shows the Pequot village attacked and destroyed by American colonists.

Massachusetts Bay Colony in 1630. These colonists were known as the Pilgrims. They were members of a religious sect that was very strict in its beliefs and had fled Britain to escape persecution from the Church of England.

The Pequot Indians, who had long inhabited the area that was to become Massachusetts, survived off the land, in harmony with nature. The new settlers wanted to clear the forests to make the land suitable for farming.

WAR WITH THE PEQUOTS

Though the Pilgrims and the Pequot Indians coexisted for a time, the Pilgrims started a war with them in 1636 over the death of a Pilgrim fur trader. Massacres occurred on both sides. The Pilgrims often killed Native American women and children during raids. They justified this with their belief that the natives were savages who had not accepted the Christian religion and were, as a result, doomed to damnation. The Pilgrims used their advanced firepower to overwhelm the Native Americans and their simple weapons.

From 1675 to 1676, the colonists fought another native tribe, the Wampanoags. The British colonists accused Metacom, the Wampanaog chief, of murder. Most colonists didn't seem to want this conflict, but leaders of the Massachusetts Bay Colony were set on taking new lands from the natives. This bloody war claimed the lives of hundreds of settlers and three thousand Wampanoags, including Metacom.

Armed conflict with the colonists was not the only peril for Native Americans during this era. Smallpox and other diseases took a terrible toll. For example, about three thousand Wampanoag lived on the island of Martha's Vineyard in 1642, when the British settled there. A short time later, only about three hundred Wampanoag were left alive. Smallpox had ravaged their population.

THE IROQUOIS LEAGUE

Well before the Europeans arrived in the Western Hemisphere, the Native Americans of what is now northern New York State had organized themselves into a single nation known as the Iroquois League. By 1722, the Cayuga, Onondaga, Oneida, Mohawk, Seneca, and Tuscarora were part of an efficient political body. Clan and village chiefs sat in councils in which every tribe had a vote.

This handwritten receipt is for land purchased from the Six Nations by the state of Pennsylvania in 1769. The payment is for $10,000. See the partial transcription on pages 53–54.

The Iroquois League fought neighboring tribes as well as the settlers of New France (in the territories north of New York, now part of Canada). They kept an uneasy peace with the British in northern New York because they traded with them.

When the thirteen colonies rebelled against the British, the league's loyalties were split. Some natives sympathized with the British because they had gone much further than the colonists in guaranteeing their lands.

The Oneida and Tuscarora fell in with the colonists, while the rest attacked American settlements on the frontier. In 1779, an expedition of four thousand American troops defeated the remaining Iroquois near Elmira, New York.

SLAVERY COMES

Another group that suffered from the colonial expansion in the New World were Africans. Kidnapped from their homes and brought to America as slaves, Africans were forced to perform menial labor and live under harsh, inhuman conditions.

The first African slaves arrived in Jamestown, Virginia, in 1619 to cultivate tobacco in the mid-Atlantic, especially around Chesapeake Bay.

Slavery grew steadily as the plantation system prospered. In 1661, a law was passed in Virginia that forbade blacks and whites from associating with each other as they had been doing in the colony for some time.

In 1700, there were about six thousand slaves living in Virginia. Slaves comprised less than 10 percent of the population. Within seventy years, slaves in Virginia numbered as many as 170,000, half of the state's population.

ESCAPE AND PUNISHMENT

By the late eighteenth century, many slaves rebelled. Some refused to do certain kinds of work, while others attempted escapes or plotted against their owners. Some slaves, newly arrived from Africa, ran off and formed their own communities on the frontier, where the English feared to go. Some escaped

This illustration from the 1845 book *A Pictorial History of the United States* depicts the confrontation between Nathaniel Bacon (*right*) and Governor William Berkeley (*left*) that occurred in 1676.

slaves found sympathy among the Native Americans who were enemies of the colonists. Some escaped slaves intermarried and became part of native tribes.

In response, many of the colonial leaders set up severe penalties for slave disobedience. Punishment included whipping, branding, torture, and often death. Punishment was made harsh to discourage attempts at escape.

For example, in 1705, Virginia declared that escaped slaves could be punished by dismemberment. Maryland passed a law in 1723 that punished slaves by cutting off their ears if they attacked their masters. Despite these cruel and frightening rules, in the mid-eighteenth century, landowners and other white colonists continued to fear slave revolts.

BACON'S REBELLION

One of the greatest nightmares of wealthy and powerful colonists was that lower-class whites would join with black slaves in revolt. This became a reality in 1676. One of the causes of Bacon's Rebellion, as this uprising was called, were issues surrounding Native Americans.

Frontiersmen in western Virginia were constantly battling the natives. They usually received little help from the aristocracy in Jamestown. The governing body of Virginia, the House of Burgesses, did little to protect them. One landowner, Nathaniel Bacon, who had fought Native Americans himself, was elected to the house in 1676. He hoped to convince Virginians to declare total war on the natives. When he didn't get help, he declared that he would organize his own forces against the Native Americans.

Virginia's governor, William Berkeley, declared Bacon a rebel and had him imprisoned. Two thousand Virginians marched on Jamestown in support of Bacon. Berkeley released him under pressure of this protest. Bacon then gathered a militia of his supporters and waged attacks on the natives. But he also was angered at the Jamestown government. He thought that its taxes were too high, its members were corrupt, and it was monopolizing trade. Bacon fought the militias rallied by Berkeley. At one point, Bacon and his group controlled much of Virginia.

The Virginians who followed Bacon were mainly disgruntled frontier farmers, servants, and other people who were struggling to make a living. Many of them had been badly affected by the failures of the corn and tobacco crops that year and resented the power of the Jamestown elite.

In one of the last battles of the conflict, a ship on the York River forced the surrender of four hundred men. Among these were blacks and whites, both slaves and servants. Poor whites who had emigrated to America as indentured servants were among the poorest of the lower class in their native England. The rebellion was finally put down after Bacon died of an unknown illness at the age of twenty-nine in the fall of 1676.

AMERICAN INDEPENDENCE

The thirteen American colonies would eventually join together as a new nation. But only through the work of slaves and poor settlers did the colonies eventually become strong enough for independence. In their drive to survive and expand, the British settlers enslaved hundreds of thousands of Africans and destroyed Native American lives and land.

By 1776, the colonies would no longer want the British to make their decisions for them. Many people in the newer generation of colonists saw England as a foreign power seeking to control them. The seeds had been planted for a break with England and the formation of a new nation. It was a new nation that showed by its internal unrest where its values really lay.

CHAPTER 3

INDIA AND THE BRITISH

The Industrial Revolution ushered in an age of mass production. Cities attracted more and more workers who left farming behind in the countryside. These changes in the eighteenth century presented Britain and other countries with a challenge. Now that they could produce cheap goods quickly, where would they sell them? Their home markets were too small.

The Industrial Revolution also brought a need for more raw materials to use in manufacturing as well as food to feed the growing European population. Colonies would help provide these needs.

A POWERFUL COMPANY

In 1600, Queen Elizabeth granted a charter (a license to operate) to the British East India Company (BEI). It would run Britain's trade with Asia. Over the next few decades, the company set up trading ports along the coast of India.

For much of the 1600s, India belonged to the Mughals, a Muslim minority that ruled a large Hindu majority. In 1627, the Mughal emperor Jahangir gave the British East India Company

This colorful seventeenth-century artwork shows the court welcoming Mughal emperor Jahangir, also known as Shah Salim.

permission to build a factory at Surat, the Mughals' most important port city.

The prosperous British East India Company set up a military branch to protect its interests. British communities formed in the major cities of Bombay, Calcutta, and Madras. As the Mughals lost influence, the British were poised to grab it. They got their chance in 1856 in Bengal.

A nawab was an aristocratic Indian ruler who headed an Indian principality. In 1756, Nawab Siraj-ud-Dawlah took over Fort William and Calcutta, which were controlled by the British East India Company. At the time, it was reported that Nawab Siraj-ud- Dawlah had imprisoned more than one hundred Englishmen in an airless jail cell of Fort William and that they had all died overnight. Although the story may have been greatly exaggerated (or never happened at all), the British believed it was true. Known as the Black Hole of Calcutta incident, it was considered an act of war.

The British were led by Robert Clive, a former civil service member who had become a military commander. They defeated Nawab Siraj-ud-Dawlah, in large part by bribing his troops. The nawab's body was found in a nearby river days after the battle.

Now Bengal, an important wealthy Indian state, was under the control of the BEI. Through a mixture of violence, more bribery, and clever negotiation, the British East India Company would slowly reshape India.

CONSOLIDATION AND CORRUPTION

Over the next few years, Robert Clive's government in Bengal was marked by great corruption. Clive required the Mughal emperor and other state officials to pay him huge sums of money. He convinced the emperor that the BEI should collect the taxes in Bengal as well as in the province of Bihar.

In response to corruption in Bengal, the British Parliament passed the Regulating Act of 1773. This placed a governor-general in Bengal who answered to Parliament instead of to the BEI. A supreme court was set up to regulate the affairs of the British in India. However, grave abuses by the court, including harsh penalties for minor crimes in the city of Calcutta, spread resentment through the colonized people.

The British underwent a period of annexation, acquiring states as buffers between their land and potential enemies. Later, they took land for the sake of power.

Between 1798 and 1805, Lord Wellesley, a governor-general, introduced the subsidiary system. Under it, the British would offer to protect a weaker neighbor against its stronger enemies. In exchange, the state would pay for the cost of the British army or give some of its land to the British.

In 1784, British prime minister William Pitt passed the India Act, which required that the BEI answer to a Board of Control

This print from 1787 shows William Pitt in the center, sitting beside two officials from the East India Company. The men were accused of receiving payments from the poor in return for getting them jobs.

ruled by the British crown. Governor-generals could now be removed by the mother country.

DISCIPLINE AND DISLOCATION

Lord Charles Cornwallis became governor-general of British India in 1786. Cornwallis banned private trade among the employees of the BEI and enforced a more rigid code of discipline. All Indian high officials were dismissed from the BEI. They were replaced by British citizens.

In addition, Cornwallis introduced British law into Bengali society, indicating that the last bit of native power was over. This made for tremendous confusion, since most Indians did not understand the British courts.

Under Cornwallis, tax and land administration were radically reformed. In Bengal, prior to British rule, a group of people called the zamindars had collected land revenue for imperial officials. The zamindars kept one-tenth of the land in exchange for their services. Many of their posts had been hereditary.

Zamindars had maintained law and order, and supplied troops in times of conflict. The new law under Cornwallis, called the Permanent Settlement of Bengal, changed a few things. Before, the land did not really "belong" to the peasants or the zamindars, even though both groups had informal hereditary ties to the lands. But the British made the zamindars into landowners, much like landlords in Britain.

Within a few years, many of the original zamindars were gone because they couldn't afford the revenues demanded by the British. They were replaced with entrepreneurs from faraway cities.

INDIAN RESISTANCE

Many Indians serving in Bengal's army under the British were angry. Since the British takeover, their wages had dropped. They lived in miserably poor conditions, often without proper sanitation or sewage. But the issue of the Lee-Enfield rifle was the last straw.

The British introduced a new Lee-Enfield rifle to their military in May 1857 in the city of Meerut, Bengal. The rifles' ammunition was packed in greased cartridges. To load this rifle, a person had to bite off the end of the cartridge.

This photo from around 1858 shows a group of Gurkha soldiers and their British officer (*center right, with sword*). The photo was taken during the Sepoy Rebellion that lasted from 1857 until 1858.

The gun makers had made a crucial cultural mistake. The material to be bitten off was made from a mixture of beef and pork. This greatly offended both Hindu and Muslim soldiers. Hindus considered cows sacred, while Muslims were not allowed to eat pork. Many of the outraged soldiers refused to accept the new cartridges and were chained for insubordination.

On May 10, 1857, fellow soldiers freed the captives who escaped to nearby Delhi. More sepoys, or Indian soldiers trained to serve under the British, joined them, and they declared the city theirs. They declared Bahadhur Shan II, the powerless Mughal emperor, their leader.

The British attempted to recall the cartridges and atone for their mistake. But it was too late. The combined British military in India, about twenty-three thousand troops, found themselves facing a native Indian revolt comprised of about three hundred thousand people. This revolt was known as the Sepoy Rebellion. It was one of the bloodiest and most shocking of all colonial wars. Both sides committed atrocities.

Though the British were initially outnumbered, reinforcements and the support of other Indians helped the British turn the tide of battle. Though their passion for freedom ran deep, the rebels were disorganized, with no aim other than to punish the British. The highly organized British took back Delhi on September 20, 1857. The British reclaimed India.

On August 2, 1858, the British Parliament passed the Government of India Act. The BEI was blamed for the revolt, and its power was transferred directly to the British crown. The power of the British East India Company was over.

EFFORTS FOR INDEPENDENCE

One of the first seeds of Indian independence was planted in December 1885, with the first meeting of the Indian National Congress (INC). Coming together were lawyers and Indian professionals who wanted a greater voice in the rule of their country. Two decades later, in 1906, the Muslim League was founded for much the same reason.

One of the most notable developments was the growing use of nonviolent resistance. It became an effective tool for the INC.

A NONVIOLENT APPROACH

One of the greatest heroes in India's struggle against British colonialism was Mohandas Gandhi, later known as Mahatma, (1869–1948). Gandhi's philosophy was rooted in nonviolence. He believed in a concept called *satyagraha*, meaning "the devotion to truth." It meant

This 1931 photo of Mahatma Gandhi was taken in London. During his travels, Gandhi made a point of wearing traditional Indian clothing and of speaking against the British presence in India.

to strive against wrongs in a nonviolent way, no matter what the cost. This included protesting through fasting and civil disobedience and accepting whatever repercussions were to come. Using nonviolence, resisters would make the oppressors, especially the violent ones, change their ways and create understanding between both parties.

Through Gandhi's efforts, the movement for Indian independence swelled. Thousands of protestors performed peaceful sit-ins, blockades, and boycotts to flood the prisons and provoke rulers. World opinion was often strongly against the British, who were perceived as barbaric in their repression of nonviolent protests.

For example, Lord Curzon attempted to split up Bengal in 1905. One side would have a Muslim majority, the other side would be mainly Hindu. The INC denounced the move as an attempt to divide and conquer the people of Bengal.

Protest spread throughout India, as the INC and other groups urged millions of people to use nonviolent resistance. Hindus in Bengal boycotted British goods and burned cloth products from Lancashire, England. Many Indians promised to wear only traditional native-made clothing. This protest extended to products such as glass and metal products. It helped reinvigorate local industry. Many people in India found great solidarity in this kind of protest.

After World War II, the dream of Indian independence became reality. At first the results were horrifying. The division of India into a majority-Hindu state (India proper) and a majority-Muslim state (Pakistan) created unprecedented violence in 1947. As millions of people migrated from one area to the other, clashes between the groups left hundreds of thousands dead. Two nations were now free to pick up the pieces of hundreds of years of colonialism.

CHAPTER 4

SOUTH AFRICA AND THE DUTCH

The European takeover of South Africa started early in the seventeenth century. That is when the Dutch East India Company created settlements off the Cape of Good Hope, the southernmost tip of the African continent. Dutch men who had worked for the company were released from their contracts in 1657. They began settling the land in the immediate area.

CULTURES CLASH

At first the Africans traded with their new Dutch visitors. Among them were the Khoikhoi and the San, groups of indigenous herders, hunters, and gatherers.

However, the Dutch and Africans soon came to blows. The Dutch kept slaves and thought themselves superior to the natives. They fought the Khoikhoi, pushing them farther inland. Natives also perished from smallpox, which the Europeans had carried with them.

The Dutch often killed the African men and enslaved the women and children. By 1800, the Dutch controlled the western edge of what is today South Africa.

CAAP DE BON ESPERA

This painting shows the Dutch fleet in the harbor of Cape Town, South Africa, around 1680. One of the official languages of South Africa is Afrikaans, which developed from the descendants of Dutch, French, and German colonists to the area.

A group of settlers who had left Cape Town to move into the frontier called themselves the Trekboers, or "wandering farmers." They lived a strict, bare existence. By the late eighteenth century, the Trekboers, or, simply, the Boers, were quickly conquering their African neighbors. They were staunch Calvinists, Christians similar to the Puritans who first colonized New England. Like colonists before and after them, the Boers considered it their divine mandate to defeat non-Christians and to tame the wilderness.

The Boers expanded into lands occupied by the Xhosa peoples, whom they fought bitterly. The Boers developed the commando system, in which small bands of guerilla fighters would strike wherever they were needed.

The Khoikhoi, living closer to Cape Town, were controlled by the Dutch who treated them harshly. A Khoikhoi who attacked a white person would be put to death by being impaled on a spear. The Dutch were so contemptuous of "colored" people that they even denied descendants of Dutch-African marriages the rights of citizenship.

THE BRITISH COME

In 1795, the British invaded the Cape region. They gained possession of the Cape colony in 1806. This was an important acquisition for Britain because of the crucial role of the Cape in trade with the Near and Far East.

The British brought more colonists, many of them arriving in 1820. This strained the already-tense situation between the Africans and the Europeans. To ease tensions between the already established Boers and new British colonists and to gain more territory, the British launched fierce attacks on neighboring Africans.

THE TREK BEGINS

The Boers at first tolerated British rule. But, like American frontiersmen, they sought new lands of their own. They also left British-ruled areas because they favored slavery, while the British had outlawed slavery in 1838.

Between 1835 and 1843, about 12,000 Boers left the main British-administered territory. This became known as the Great Trek. They took over land using their superior weapons and making military pacts with the powerful tribes they encountered. Whenever the British attempted to interfere in affairs between the Boers and the independent natives on this northern frontier, it led to more bloodshed. The British withdrew for a time and granted independence to the two new Boer states that had been established, Transvaal and the Orange Free State.

Both Boer states instituted the strict regime of what later was known as apartheid. Meaning "apartness" in the Boers' language, Afrikaans, apartheid meant that whites and nonwhites were to be strictly segregated, or separated, in both church and state. This usually meant that the nonwhites lived under far worse conditions and oppression. This policy would last well into the modern era.

THE BOER WARS

The Boers and British expanded their power over their African neighbors. But the discovery of gold, diamonds, and other precious materials set the stage for eventual war between the two groups.

The discovery of diamonds in 1867 on the frontier brought mining to northern South Africa. The British soon moved to annex the whole area as part of a British-controlled federation. By the end of the nineteenth century, a large group of mainly English settlers had come to Transvaal, now called the South African Republic. These were the Utlanders. The British wanted the Boers to grant political rights to these settlers, who had come to mine gold in the region.

This photo from 1896 shows Boer soldiers riding through an unnamed South African town. The Boers bitterly resented fortune hunters who came to the country when diamonds and gold were discovered there.

The Boers of the South African Republic and the Orange Free State did not comply. On October 11, 1899, the Boers declared war on the British because the British had reinforced a military garrison (or base) and the Boers took this as a threat against them. Half a million British faced off against only eighty-eight thousand Boers.

Despite early Boer victories, the British gained the upper hand. One British general, Lord Kitchener, made a ruthless bid to crush the Boers. Kitchener's forces burned and pillaged Boer towns and villages, along with those of Africans. Thousands of Boers were placed in concentration camps, where more than twenty thousand women and children perished. The Boer commandos, though they were scoring small and occasional victories, were eventually forced to surrender.

The Peace of Vereeneging in 1902 ended the Boer War. The Boers were disarmed, and the British military took over the South African Republic and the Orange Free State. The British made one concession to the Boers, however. They agreed to delay voting rights for nonwhites until after the Boers had established their own government. This sealed the fate of nonwhites in South Africa for decades.

APARTHEID IN THE TWENTIETH CENTURY

The Union of South Africa was established on May 31, 1910, and it brought the entire region together for the first time. Under the new constitution, Africans were given no power. Apartheid became the official system of the new society.

The population of the union was made up of the Boers, also known as Afrikaners; the British; and the African majority. Even in the more liberal territory of the Cape, only whites could hold political office. As of 1910, only 5 percent of the African population could vote.

Over time, the Afrikaners' influence grew. Afrikaans became South Africa's official language in 1925, replacing Dutch.

By 1931, the Statute of Westminster in the British Parliament gave full independence to South Africa. In the following years, whites increased their power. The government provided money and other support to white farmers, with the aim of lifting all whites out of poverty. Blacks were prevented from holding better jobs. In 1936, the few nonwhites with voting rights had them taken away by Parliament.

The standard of living jumped for whites as South Africa became an economic power at the end of the 1930s. It stayed the same or worsened for nonwhites, which included Africans and the large Indian population.

AFRICANS DEMAND TO BE HEARD

In 1950, Parliament passed further laws to separate the people by color. The Population Registration Act classified every resident of the nation according to race. Interracial marriage or sexual relations were strictly prohibited. Africans could not go to the same hotels, movies, restaurants, or even funeral homes as whites. Police could also arrest and imprison blacks without trial or legal representation under laws enacted later.

In 1951, the South African government set up the Natives Representatives Council to oversee "homelands" that grouped the Africans living in the countryside into separate areas. The chiefs of these homelands were often handpicked by the white government and were easily controlled by them.

By the 1970s, South Africa was among the most modern and wealthy nations on the continent. But the whites, comprising a fifth of the population, held great power over the remaining four-fifths of nonwhites who provided most of the labor and services.

In response to apartheid, a new political movement sprang up among the African majority. This was the South African Native National Congress, which later became the African National Congress (ANC). This group would play a major role in the struggle for black self-determination.

By the 1960s, the protest movement among the native Africans was growing. An African lawyer, Nelson Mandela, and other leaders provided the inspiration for protesters. The

A barefoot woman carries a child through the South African shantytown of Moroka, Johannesburg, in 1950. The daily lives of blacks differed sharply from those of whites.

Pan-Africanist Congress (PAC), led by a university teacher named Robert Sobukwe, launched a protest in March 1960 in which thousands subjected themselves to arrest by arriving at police stations without identification passes, which was against

SLEGS BLANKE
EUROPEANS ONL

This 1952 photo shows black South Africans defying laws segregating the races and confining blacks to separate train cars. The protestors chanted "Africa" and gave the thumbs-up sign before officials removed them from the train.

the law. At one demonstration near the city of Johannesburg, police fired into the crowds, killing sixty-seven people. Later they arrested up to eleven thousand people.

The ANC and PAC changed their tactics and started committing terrorist acts, bombing government buildings. Both Nelson Mandela and Robert Sobukwe were arrested by the government and sentenced to long prison terms. The ANC and other antiapartheid groups were banned.

FREEDOM!

Throughout the 1980s, political pressure from around the world and from within South Africa made real change possible. Mandela and other leaders, including Anglican Archbishop Desmond Tutu, continued to be a voice against apartheid. Large strikes and nonviolent protests forced the hand of the South African government. In 1989, F. W. de Klerk, a leader of the Transvaal region, was elected as leader of the ruling National Party and the country. Two years later, he announced a system of radical reforms: the repeal of many apartheid laws, a general political amnesty, and the freeing of Nelson Mandela on February 11, 1990.

In 1994, the African National Congress won the first elections in which all citizens were allowed to vote. The long road to freedom had been hard fought and a long time coming. Members of the black majority who had been left out of the freedom and prosperity of their own country for so long now finally had their voice.

CHAPTER 5

THE FRENCH AND VIETNAM

The first Westerners to live among the Vietnamese were Catholic missionaries. Their presence had been generally peaceful until a rebellion in 1777. The Tay Son insurgency swept the House of Nguyen from power, massacring the entire royal family except for Prince Nguyen Anh. The prince escaped to Phu Quoc Island, where Catholic missionaries urged him to ask the French for help against the Tay Son regime.

RELIGIOUS DISAGREEMENT AND INVASION

On August 17, 1798, the Tay Son ruler, King Canh Thinh, ordered the destruction of all Catholic churches and missions. Persecution lasted until Prince Nguyen was restored as ruler. Remembering the aid given him by the Catholics, he reinstated their freedom of religion.

However, the presence of Catholicism worried many Vietnamese, including Chinese Confucians who struggled against the French in Nguyen's government.

Nguyen's firstborn son, Prince Canh, had been educated in France. The French hoped that Catholicism would spread during his rule and westernize Vietnam. The Chinese faction supported his younger brother, Prince Mien Tong.

This April 1859 engraving shows a combined force of Spanish and French soldiers attacking the citadel of Saigon in Vietnam. The assault took place on February 17, 1859.

But French influence soon collapsed. Prince Canh is said to have died from the measles at the age of twenty-one, although French missionaries reported that he had been poisoned.

Mien Tong was crowned Emperor Minh Mang. Canh's followers were stripped of their powers. Some were executed.

In France, resentment grew against the anti-Christian attitude in Vietnam. The Vietnamese, cutting off most contact with the world at large, expelled many missionaries. The conservative Confucians resisted change. However, the country stagnated, falling victim to corruption and the breakdown of government.

In 1858, a French expedition landed at Tourane (present-day Danang), requesting permission to set up a consulate and a trading office. When the emperor turned the men down, the French took Tourane by force.

The French found a country that was ill equipped to protect itself. In 1859, France captured the city of Gia Dinh (later known as Saigon and Ho Chi Minh City).

Why did the French want Vietnam? Their motivations were similar to other colonizers. France needed raw materials and markets for their products. Plus, the French felt that their culture was superior to that of Vietnam. They considered it their moral duty to educate people in "unfortunate" regions of the world. Their "refinement" and "humanity" were forced on people at the barrel of a gun.

After a series of battles, the French claimed the areas surrounding Gia Dinh. By June 1862, the Vietnamese emperor, Tu Duc, was forced to sign the Treaty of Saigon.

Tu Duc gave up much of the south, enabling the French to sail their warships up the Mekong River into Cambodia. He also paid the French large sums of money. The French forced neighboring Cambodia to give up some provinces as well.

Soon, the French took the city of Hanoi. Another treaty was forced on Tu Duc in which the Vietnamese emperor was forced to accept that the French had "full and entire sovereignty" over North Vietnam.

The capital city of Hue fell in August 1883. Tu Duc himself was not around to see his nation's defeat: he had died a month earlier. North and central Vietnam now belonged to the French. The new emperor was a figurehead.

THE RULING CLASS

In 1887, the French created the Indochinese Union, which included south and north Vietnam, central Vietnam and Cambodia, and Laos.

This 1867 photo of the Saigon bay shows traditional ships in the foreground and European-style buildings under construction in the background.

Frenchmen filled all the important posts in the government. A few Vietnamese officials, left over from the emperor's government, collaborated with the French, but they had no real power.

Vietnamese who wanted to travel through the country needed to carry identification. The Vietnamese were not allowed freedom of assembly or freedom of the press. French magistrates could imprison people at will. Like other colonized peoples, the Vietnamese were forced to labor, called corvée.

By 1925, there were about five thousand French officials in government posts. They oversaw a native Vietnamese population of about thirty million people.

The French built highways, bridges, canals, and other infrastructure, which helped them remove the vast natural resources including rubber, minerals, and coal from the region. They also exported rice from Vietnam, leaving many Vietnamese to starve.

Some Vietnamese remained landholders under French rule, including Vietnamese Catholics who collaborated with the French. The lion's share of the land was given to French colonists, called colons. A handful of landlords oversaw a landless peasantry, who were so highly taxed that they were reduced to poverty. The French also controlled most industry. They owned more than 90 percent of the rubber plantations in Vietnam.

Some reforms were instituted by France, but enforcing them overseas was nearly impossible. Most colonial officials ignored the new rules.

RESISTANCE AND REBELLION

Discontent brewed among the Vietnamese. They clung in private to traditional education based on classic Chinese texts. Anticolonial ideas had begun to surface in their literature.

Though the French controlled the government and exploited Vietnam for its wealth, they could not crush the spirit of the Vietnamese. Resistance leadership, mostly scholars, emerged from the ranks of the old government. One of the most respected men was Phan Boi Chau. A firsthand witness to French oppression, Chau traveled through Vietnam trying to muster the remnants of a rebel movement called the Can Vuoung (which means "Save the King"). Chau believed a nationalist movement could restore the monarchy to Vietnam. In 1904, he formed the Duy Tan Hoi, or the "Reformation Society."

Chau, who was deported, spent time wandering in Asia, preaching resistance from abroad. His efforts against the French grew more desperate. He helped coordinate assassinations and terrorist bombings. The French had him arrested and imprisoned by the Chinese between 1914 and 1917. Later freed, he was kidnapped by French agents in Shanghai, China, to face trial in Hanoi. He died under house arrest in 1940.

Another nationalist, anticolonial movement rose in 1925 when a young sailor named Nguyen Ai Quoc formed the Revolutionary

This 1954 photo shows French captives writing letters home as they sit under a portrait of Viet Minh leader Ho Chi Minh. Communist "peace doves" decorate the wall on either side of the portrait.

Youth League of Vietnam. A world traveler, he had become a Communist in Paris. The Communist movement believed that the working people in a country should own all industry and property together and benefit from it. It sought to do away with what it saw as the evils of capitalism—the rich taking advantage of the poor.

By 1930, Quoc, later known as Ho Chi Minh (which means "He Who Enlightens"), formed the Vietnamese Communist Party. Later, during World War II, the Communist Party joined with other groups to form the Viet Minh, or the League for the Independence of Vietnam. After the war, Ho Chi Minh led talks with the French in which the Viet Minh hoped to secure an independent state. However, the two sides could not agree. When a French naval attack on the port city of Haiphong killed thousands, the First Indochina War (also called the French Indochina War) began.

GUERILLA WARFARE

The Viet Minh, led by Ho Chi Minh, fought a guerilla war against the French. When China became Communist in 1949, it, too, aided the Vietnamese Communists. The United States, at the time embroiled in the Cold War with the Soviet Union, feared what would happen if Vietnam became a Communist nation, supported the French.

The rebels captured a French military garrison at Dien Bien Phu in May 1954. In July 1954, the conflict reached a cease-fire. To reach a settlement, Switzerland, France, and the Democratic Republic of Vietnam met in Geneva. The French were ordered to keep their forces in the south, while the Viet Minh were allowed to keep their land in the north. National elections were set for July 1956 to decide which direction the country would take.

The elections never took place. Eventually, the split between north and south escalated into war again. The United States

This April 1975 photo shows the fall of Saigon to the North Vietnamese Communists. Desperate citizens tried to escape the city, helped by American soldiers.

supported the south once more, while Communist nations fell in with the north. A full decade of war, with millions of Vietnamese dead on both sides, as well as more than fifty thousand US soldiers killed, ended in 1975 with the fall of Saigon, the capital of the southern government. The long road to Vietnamese reunification was over, and the Communists had prevailed.

THE EFFECTS OF COLONIALISM

Although European colonialism is, in large measure, part of the past, its aftereffects run deep. In 1894, Lord Curzon, the Viceroy of British India, said, "India is the pivot of our Empire … if we lose

India, the sun of our Empire will have set." Today, historians are looking beyond the age-old myth that colonialism improves the lives of "savages." Instead, many scholars are examining the callous attitudes of colonizers toward the people they colonized.

In India, for example, the British government ignored the growing poverty and hardship of the people whose country they were occupying. Records show that life expectancy for Indians in British India between 1872 and 1931 fell from fifty-five to twenty-three years, as Indian lives were dramatically shortened by increased squalor, famine, and disease. Meanwhile, the British were pumping Indian resources, or the profits they earned, into the mother country.

As a result of British colonialism, India's Hindu majority, Muslim minority, and the people of countless other cultures are now linked by speaking English, the language of commerce, science, and of the computer era. However, the British in India ignored the educational needs of the Indian people, creating a pattern of neglect that keeps them struggling today.

In 1911, the literacy rate in British India had been 6 percent. It inched to 8 percent by 1931. By 1935, still only four out of ten thousand people attended a university or school of higher education. By 1995, literacy in India had bounced to 52 percent. But is has much further to go.

In Latin America, most people speak Spanish, share similar cuisine and music, and are members of the Catholic Church. In parts of the Caribbean, the descendants of former slaves have melded old African faiths with the worship of Catholic saints. But millions of lives and many cultures and languages were lost along the way.

The long-term strife created by colonialism can be seen in today's headlines. The nation of Iraq, for example, is not actually a country with a single culture and ethnicity, like a nation such as Poland. Instead, Iraq is a collection of minority groups. Shiite, Sunni Muslims, and Kurds have very little in common with each other. Iraq has existed as a sovereign (independent) nation only since 1932. The British claimed it after the defeat of the Ottoman Empire in World War I.

Racial tensions continue to flare throughout the world in a landscape where colonizers and native people struggle to coexist in a postcolonial reality. On the continent of Africa, new boundaries were created by colonizers for their own convenience. Often, tribes or nations that had been brutal enemies for centuries were forced to live together.

To get beyond the long shadows of colonialism, people must work to understand and respect each other's cultures and rights. People must take the positive remnants of colonialism, and leave behind its negative by-products.

TIMELINE

1492	Christopher Columbus discovers the New World.
1493	Pope Alexander VI issues the Inter Caetera.
1494	The Treaty of Tordesillas is issued.
1531	Francisco Pizarro and his men defeat the Incas.
1541	The New Laws are issued by the Spanish crown.
1600	The British East India Company is incorporated.
1627	The Mughal ruler of India gives the British East India Company permission to build an office in the port city of Surat.
1773	The British pass the Regulating Act.
1777	Vietnamese prince Nguyen Anh is deposed by a revolt.
1784	British prime minister William Pitt passes the India Act.
1821	Peru gains its independence from Spain.
1857	The Sepoy Rebellion occurs.
1883	The French take the Vietnamese capital of Hue and now rule Vietnam.
1885	The Indian National Congress is formed to seek self-determination for Indians in their own country.
1947	India is freed from British rule.
1975	Saigon falls to the North Vietnamese.

Treaty between Spain and Portugal concluded at Tordesillas; June 7, 1494
Partial Transcription

Whereas a certain controversy exists between the said lords, their constituents, as to what lands, of all those discovered in the ocean sea up to the present day, the date of this treaty, pertain to each one of the said parts respectively; therefore, for the sake of peace and concord, and for the preservation of the relationship and love of the said King of Portugal for the said King and Queen of Castile, Aragon, etc. it being the pleasure of their Highnesses, they ... covenanted and agreed that a boundary or straight line be determined and drawn north and south, from pole to pole, on the said ocean sea, from the Arctic to the Antarctic pole. This boundary or line shall be drawn straight, as aforesaid, at a distant of three hundred and seventy leagues west of the Cape Verde Islands, being calculated by degrees ... And all lands, both islands and mainlands, found and discovered already, or to be found and discovered hereafter, by the said King of Portugal and by his vessels on this side of the said line and bound determined as above, toward the east, in either north or south latitude, on the eastern side of the said bound, provided the said bound is not crossed, shall belong to and remain in the possession of, and pertain forever to, the said King of Portugal and his successors. And all other lands, both islands and mainlands, found or to be found hereafter ... by the said King and Queen of Castile, Aragon, etc. and by their vessels, on the western side of the said bound, determined as above, after having passed the said bound toward the west, in either its north or south latitude, shall belong to ... the said King and Queen of Castile, Leon, etc. and to their successors.

Receipt for lands sold by the Treaty of Fort Stanwix to Iroquois League
Partial Transcription

s.l., 28 July 1769.

Received from the honorable Thomas and Richard Penn Esqrs. true and absolute Proprietaries of Pennsylvania by the hands of the honorable Sir William Johnson Baronet the sum of ten thousand Dollars being the full consideration of the Lands lately sold to them by the Indians of the six Nations at the late Treaty of Fort Stanwix We say received this Twenty Eighth day of July—Anno

Domini 1769—for ourselves and the other Indians of the six Nations and their confederates and dependant Tribes for whom we act and by whom we are appointed and empowered—

Statement by President Gerald Ford about American withdrawal from Saigon.
Partial Transcription

FOR IMMEDIATE RELEASE   APRIL 29, 1975

OFFICE OF THE WHITE HOUSE PRESS SECRETARY
THE WHITE HOUSE
STATEMENT BY THE PRESIDENT

During the past week, I had ordered the reduction of American personnel in the United States mission in Saigon to levels that could be quickly evacuated during an emergency, while enabling the mission to continue to fulfill its duties.

During the day on Monday, Washington time, the airport at Saigon came under persistent rocket as well as artillery fire and was effectively closed. The military situation in the area deteriorated rapidly.

I, therefore, ordered the evacuation of all American military personnel remaining in South Viet Nam.

The evacuation has been completed … this action closes a chapter in the American experience. I ask all Americans to close ranks, to avoid recrimination about the past, to look ahead to the many goals we share and to work together on the great tasks that remain to be accomplished.

COLONIALISM An economic, social, and political system in which colonies are used by conquering nations as sources of economic and military advantage.

COLONY A territory that has been settled by people from another country and is controlled by that country.

CONQUISTADOR Spanish explorers and conquerors of much of Central and South America starting in the fifteenth century.

DIVAN The system of taxation and monetary tribute in India prior to British rule.

ENCOMENDERO The owner or ruler of an encomienda

ENCOMIENDA A piece of land in Spain's colonies in the New World, controlled by a Spaniard who had power over any native people that lived on that land.

HINDUISM The dominant religion in India.

INCA A people native to South America whose empire was conquered by the Spanish in the sixteenth century.

MUGHALS A Muslim people that ruled much of India before the British took over.

NAWAB An Indian prince.

PAPAL BULL A decree by the pope or by the Catholic Church.

PARTITION OF INDIA The separation of the Indian subcontinent in 1947 into the predominantly Hindu nation of India and the predominantly Muslim nation of Pakistan.

SEPOYS Indian soldiers that served under the command of the British military.

American Museum of Natural History
Central Park West at 79th Street
New York, NY 10024-5192
(212) 769-5100
Website: https://www.amnh.org/exhibitions/permanent
exhibitions/human-origins-and-cultural-halls/hall-of-mexico
   -and-central-america
Facebook: @naturalhistory
Twitter and Instagram: @amnh
Learn about the indigenous culture of Latin America by visiting
   the Hall of Mexico and Central America, which includes the
   20-ton (18–metric ton) Aztec Stone of the Sun, gold objects,
   jeweled sculptures, and more.

Canadian Museum of History
100 Laurier Street
Gatineau, QC K1A 0M8
Canada
(800) 555-5621
Website: http://www.historymuseum.ca
Facebook, Twitter, and Instagram: @CanMusHistory
The museum features exhibits on the government and founding
   of Canada, a country with strong colonial ties to both England
   and France.

Canadian War Museum
1 Vimy Place
Ottawa, ON K1A 0M8
Canada
(800) 555-5621

Website: http://www.warmuseum.ca
Facebook: @warmuseum
Twitter: @CanWarMuseum
Instagram: @canwarmuseum
This museum features Canada's involvement in armed conflicts
    and its interaction with monarchies in Britain.

Library of Congress
101 Independence Avenue, SE
Washington, DC 20540
(202) 707-5000
Website: http://www.loc.gov
Facebook: @libraryofcongress
Twitter and Instagram: @librarycongress
Multiple collections reveal American history in art, documents,
    and artifacts from the exploration to the political foundation
    of the Americas.

Mariners' Museum and Park
100 Museum Drive
Newport News, VA 23606
(757) 596-2222
Website: https://exploration.marinersmuseum.org
Facebook, Twitter, and Instagram: @marinersmuseum
The museum has been designated by Congress as America's
    National Maritime Museum. Explorers from the Age of
    Discovery are a special focus.

Metropolitan Museum of Art
1000 Fifth Avenue
New York, NY 10028
(212) 535-7710
Website: https://www.metmuseum.org
Facebook, Twitter, and Instagram: @metmuseum

The museum's exhibitions contain art from cultures across the globe.

National Museum of the American Indian
Fourth Street & Independence Avenue, SW
Washington, DC 20560
(202) 633-1000
Email: nmai-info@si.edu
Website: http://www.nmai.si.edu
Facebook: @NationalMuseumoftheAmericanIndianTwitter
Instagram: @SmithsonianNMAI
A member of the Smithsonian Institutes, the museum includes one of the largest collections of Native American artifacts, photographs, and archives comprising the entire Western Hemisphere.

Beckman, Rosina. *Colonial and Postcolonial Africa*. New York, NY: Britannica Educational Publishing, 2017.

Chandler, Julia. *Colonial and Postcolonial East and Southeast Asia*. New York, NY: Britannica Educational Publishing, 2017.

Clarke, Catriona, Adam Larkum, Laura Parker, and Josephine Thompson. *Aztecs*. London, UK: Usborne, 2015.

Dawson, Patricia. *First Peoples of the Americas and the European Age of Exploration*. New York, NY: Cavendish Square Publishing, 2016.

Day, Meredith. *The Colonial and Postcolonial Middle East*. New York, NY: Britannica Educational Publishing, 2017.

Duignan, Brian. *Forms of Government and the Rise of Democracy*. New York, NY: Rosen Publishing, 2013.

Mooney, Carla, and Tom Casteel. *Explorers of the New World: Discover the Golden Age of Exploration*. White River Junction, VT: Nomad Press, 2011.

Pletcher, Kenneth. *The Age of Exploration: From Christopher Columbus to Ferdinand Magellan*. New York, NY: Britannica Educational Publishing, 2014.

Witmer, Scott. *Political Systems*. Oxford, UK: Capstone Global Library Ltd., 2013.

Wolfe, James. *The Colonial Period*. New York, NY: Britannica Educational Publishing, 2016.

BIBLIOGRAPHY

Césaire, Aimé. *Discourse on Colonialism*. New York, NY: Monthly Review Press, 1972.

Curtin, Philip D. *The World and the West: The European Challenge and the Overseas Response in the Age of Empire*. Cambridge, UK: Cambridge University Press, 2000.

Docs Teach. "Statement by the President on Evacuation of American Personnel from South Viet Nam 4/29/1975." Retrieved on May 22, 2018. https://www.docsteach.org /documents/document/president-evacuation-south-vietnam.

Gilder Lehrman Institute of American History. "Receipt for Land Purchased from the Six Nations, 1769." Retrieved on May 22, 2018. https://www.gilderlehrman.org/content /receipt-land-purchased-six-nations-1769.

Kiernan, V. G. *The Lords of Human Kind: Black Man, Yellow Man, and White Man in an Age of Empire*. Boston, MA: Little, Brown and Company, 1969.

Marshall, P. J., ed. *The Cambridge Illustrated History of the British Empire*. Cambridge, UK: Cambridge University Press, 1996.

Osterhammel, Jürgen. *Colonialism: A Theoretical Overview*. Princeton, NJ: Markus Wiener Publishers, 1997.

Sowell, Thomas. *Conquests and Cultures: An International History*. New York, NY: Basic Books, 1999.

University of Groningen. "The Treaty of Tordesillas June 7 1494." Retrieved on May 22, 2018. http://www.let.rug.nl/usa /documents/before-1600/the-treaty-of-tordesillas -june-7-1494.php.

INDEX

ABOUT THE AUTHORS

Xina M. Uhl discovered her love of history while still in grade school. She went on to obtain a master of arts in history from California State University, Northridge. She has authored books, textbooks, teacher's guides, lessons, and assessment questions in the field of history.

Philip Wolny is an author and editor from Queens, New York. His titles include *Native American Treatment and Resistance, The New Nation,* and *The Underground Railroad: A Primary Source History of the Journey to Freedom,* among others. He resides in New York City with his wife and daughter.

PHOTO CREDITS

Cover (Christopher Columbus) Everett Historical/Shutterstock.com; cover (Constitution) iStock.com/CastaldoStudio; cover (historic map) I. Pilon/Shutterstock.com; p. 5 Culture Club/Hulton Archive /Getty Images; p. 7 Amy Corti/Shutterstock.com; p. 9 Alberto Paredes /Alamy Stock Photo; p. 12 DEA/Biblioteca Ambrosiana/De Agostini /Getty Images; p. 15 Everett Collection Inc./Alamy Stock Photo; p. 16 Library of Congress Rare Book and Special Collections; p. 18 © North Wind Picture Archives; p. 20 Interim Archives/Archive Photos /Getty Images; p. 24 Institute of Oriental Studies, St. Petersburg, Russia/Bridgeman Images; p. 26 Hulton Archive/Getty Images; p. 28 Science & Society Picture Library/Getty Images; p. 30 ullstein bild /Getty Images; p. 33 Print Collector/Hulton Fine Art Collection /Getty Images; pp. 36, 45 Wellcome Collection, CC BY; p. 39 Margaret Bourke-White/The LIFE Picture Collection/Getty Images; pp. 40, 47 Bettmann/Getty Images; p. 43 DEA Picture Library/De Agostini /Getty Images; p. 49 Dirck Halstead/Hulton Archive/Getty Images; chapter opener pages (world map silhouette) Vectorios2016 /DigitalVision Vectors/Getty Images.

Design and Layout: Nicole Russo-Duca; Photo Researcher: Nicole DiMella